HEY DONALD

Trump's First 100 Days

In 100 Letters

Kevin Fristad

ISBN - 13: 978-1546513988

DEDICATED TO

ALL THOSE WHO ARE TRYING

TO MAKE THEIR VOICES HEARD

INTRODUCTION

On the evening of January 19, 2017, the day before the Presidential Inauguration, I attended a local event sponsored by "The Ghostlight Project". Thousands of people gathered outside theaters across America to, "join in a collective, simultaneous action, together creating light for challenging times ahead."

We were asked to "make a pledge to stand for and protect the values of inclusion, participation, and compassion for everyone." I decided at that moment to write a letter each day for awhile to our newly elected President. I sent my first letter on Inauguration Day and my last one 100 days later.

My reasons were several. The first was obviously to state my views in a tangible way by channeling the rage, anger, fear, and sadness I felt after Donald Trump's election. Secondly, by posting them on Facebook, I hoped to expose a few issues that are not easily found in the regular press. Finally, I thought I might be able to perhaps inspire others to contact their elected officials on a regular basis.

So what is the best way to register dissent, and how best can we affect change for the good? It all begins within. We must take the time to educate ourselves and others - and then we need to become far more involved than ever.

Now is the time to raise the volume and let our elected officials know in no uncertain terms who holds the power.

We do.

SUBJECTS

1/20/17

Hey Donald,

I just watched the inauguration.

As NBC News commented immediately following your speech, "it was surprisingly divisive", and was insulting to every former President sitting there as well as all elected officials in attendance - both Republican and Democrat. I agree.

I was hoping you would have taken the high road and done your best to bring the country together. Instead you seemed to speak only to your base.

Oh, and why did you scowl so much? You seemed really angry much of the time.

Nevertheless, it was good to see a peaceful transfer of power.

I did not vote for you and I believe you are way in over your head.

However, I wish you well. You will be hearing from me often.

I will try to keep my letters short to accommodate your attention span.

1/21/17

Hey Donald,

A lot of women came out to send a message to you today. If I were you, I would take notice. They're not very happy.

Do you remember when you said this in 2005:

"I'm automatically attracted to beautiful women — I just start kissing them, it's like a magnet. Just kiss. I don't even wait. And when you're a star, they let you do it. You can do anything, grab 'em by the pussy."

So, did you notice all of the pink "pussy hats". It appears that you started a new trend.

I have a friend who makes them, so if you think Melania would like one, I'm sure I can get my friend to make her one. Just let me know.

Or maybe you would like one too? You could wear it to one of your press conferences. It might be kind of fun.

Anyway, should be an interesting 4 years.

1/22/17

Hey Donald,

So I saw that you went to the CIA yesterday and spoke in front of the stars representing those brave service men and women who gave their lives for our country.

Thank you for finally saying some good things about the CIA.

However, much of your speech (which we thought would be all about mending fences and honoring those brave citizens who were killed in action), was aimed at the press for being dishonest.

And once again you indulged in self aggrandizement - at the CIA, no less! Dude! What's that about?

Yes, you ripped the press for reporting the truth (or what you considered to be lies) about the crowd size at your inauguration.

Please try not to feel insecure about the number of people who like or don't like you. It's petty, really.

Then this morning I watched Kellyanne Conway refer to Sean Spicer's untruths about the size of the inauguration crowd on Friday as "alternative facts". Boy, that's a new one.

1/23/17

Hey Donald,

I know that you really like polls and believe in them, or at least you used to believe in them until you won the election! I guess you showed 'em. They sure were wrong, weren't they :)

OK so for whatever it's worth, there's a new WaPo/ABC poll out now that says that 74% of Americans including 53% of Republicans think you should release your taxes.

But.... Kellyanne said yesterday that you will not be releasing your returns because "people don't care". Hey, I care!

Do you remember during the campaign that you said you would release them once the IRS was done auditing you? Are they done? Come on, Man, what is there to hide? You promised!

Maybe the lawsuit that Citizens for Responsibility and Ethics filed today will force you to open up. I'm sure you've heard about it - something having to do with the Emoluments Clause, whatever that is. These lawyers are smart (like you), so I guess they'll figure it out.

1/24/17

Hey Donald,

Somebody in today's the paper wrote, "the sorest winner of all time cannot stop whining". It's true - Jeez, man give it up!!!!!

So last night you said that 5 million illegal votes caused you to lose the popular election. Everyone but you knows that's a lie. You're the President now - you're supposed to be a big boy!

And then you sent Sean Spicer out to hammer the press about your crowd size. (Obama's was much larger than yours). Did you know that Fidel Castro behaved like that around this same issue? Apparently he had the same insecurities you do.

Some of your people apparently confided with Ashley Parker, Philip Rucker and Matea Gold last night, and here's what they wrote: "Trump has been resentful, even furious, at what he views as the media's failure to reflect the magnitude of his achievements, and he feels demoralized that the public's perception of his presidency so far does not necessarily align with his own sense of accomplishment".

I am seriously worried about your ability to maintain your composure during an International crisis. Seriously....

1/25/17

Hey Donald,

I think it's important to not only criticize things you don't like, but also to let politicians know when you like what they do.

You met with labor leaders yesterday. As a Republican, that was ballsy, so kudos, my friend!

Then, in resurrecting the Keystone and Dakota Access pipelines (bad, but that's another issue), you directed that all future pipelines would be made from US manufactured steel. Good for you here too, Pal. It's about time!

So I have a question - why did you use Chinese made steel and aluminum for "The Trump International Hotel Las Vegas" and "The Trump International Hotel & Tower Chicago"? And then according to Newsweek, you tried to cover it up! Huh?

Also, why are your neckties made in China? I saw pictures on Google Images (pictures don't lie) of a tie with your insignia, "Donald J. Trump Signature Collection" right next to another one with the words, "Hecho En China" (Made in China).

With all of your talk about China stealing our jobs, don't you think it's important that as President, you set an example?

1/26/17

Hey Donald,

Man, you are embarrassing me!!! I just watched your very first interview as President on ABC last night and was stunned by your cluelessness. I hate to say its, but you are blowing your presidency and you've only been in office for 6 days!

Give up the crowd thing! I'm trying not to swear, but it's hard....

Torture? It will be interesting to watch you and John McCain on the mat on this one. John's going to win, you know. And maybe you weren't listening when they talked about waterboarding, but both Pompeo and Mattis are not on your same planet with this issue - they're on Earth. Where the heck are you?

And your blustering about your CIA speech. Of course, Fox is going to say it was a great speech - they're saying things you want to hear because then you will like them. Standing ovation? I heard you brought in your people to do the clapping. Is that true? I read that a lot of CIA peeps were shaking their heads.

Oh, and the 5 million illegals costing you the popular vote? How are you going to feel when the results of your voter fraud investigation prove you wrong? Well, you'll probably just call them liars the way things are going. God and Goddess, help us...

1/27/17

Hey Donald,

You just reinstated the Mexico City Policy. It was a criminal act and I doubt that you even read it. They tell me you seldom read anything.

Basically you are killing women with this action. And pathetically a whole bunch of white men stood around and watched.

This thing cuts off access to contraceptives, makes cancer screenings harder to get, undermines vaccination campaigns (oh, that's right, you're an antivaxer), and will allow HIV and the Zika Virus to spread. Women will die....AND, abortions will increase!

This was proven after Bush signed the same order, but you went even further. Marie Stopes International (look them up) says that if they cannot find replacement funding, this new policy will result in 6.5 million unintentional pregnancies, 2.1 million unsafe abortions and 21,700 women dying. Yes, 21,700.

These victims are voiceless and powerless. After Bush did this, a young woman in Ghana named Kolgu Inusah got pregnant and she tried to abort herself using herbs, but it went bad. She suffered immeasurable pain and then died, leaving 2 children without their Mom. Think about it.

1/28/17

Hey Donald,

I think the most disturbing thing to me and a lot of people is that you cannot tell fact from fiction. Quite simply, you're delusional.

At the CIA you said this about your inauguration, "It was almost raining, but God looked down and he said, we're not going to let it rain on your speech. In fact, when I first started, I said, oh, no. The first line, I got hit by a couple of drops. And I said, oh, this is too bad, but we'll go right through it. But the truth is that it stopped immediately. It was amazing. And then it became really sunny. And then I walked off and it poured right after I left. It poured."

No Sir. It did rain on you. We saw it on TV. Franklin Graham even said so. The sun never came out. It did not get "really sunny". It did not pour after you got off the stage. Even God knows this. And for good measure, the satellite images prove it.

There are a bunch of examples like this since you became a candidate and now President.

So we are left to wonder if you really know that you are lying when you say off-the-wall stuff like this, or if you really don't know the difference. Most of us are now realizing that it's the latter and it's scary as hell.

1/29/17

Hey Donald,

You created thousands of terrorists worldwide on Friday. You keep saying how smart you are. How smart is that? The repercussions from your immigration ban will be extraordinary.

Get this - according to the Cato Institute, between 1975 and 2015, no one has been killed on American soil by a terrorist from the countries you slammed the door on - Iran, Iraq, Libya, Somalia, Sudan, Syria, and Yemen. The current vetting is intense. You've made a hateful and disgusting mountain out of a molehill.

But....none of the hijackers on 9/11 were from those countries! They came from Saudi Arabia, the UAE, Egypt and Lebanon. Why weren't those countries banned too? I can tell you why - you have business interests in each of them, according to NPR.

Thankfully the ACLU, stepped in and slapped you down. The courts are our only beacon of hope now. Many Congressional Republicans are writhing in dismay at your antics, but are terrified at getting tweeted out of office by you.

As Misha Pinkhasov wrote, "While we wait for a GOP mutiny, they keep giving their useful idiot just enough rope to hang himself." It appears that it's just a matter of time....

1/30/17

Hey Donald,

Yesterday I wrote that you created thousands more terrorists. Well, they are now celebrating, saying that your new policy validates their claim that the US is at war with Islam.

One said online that you were "the best caller to Islam".

ISIS leader, Abu Bakr al Baghdadi calls this a "blessed ban".

If you want to get rid of ISIS like you keep saying, you just made your job much, much harder. Do you ever think things through?

Robert Richer who worked for the CIA for 35 years in counterterrorism called your action a "strategic mistake" saying that it "was a win for jihadists and other anti-U.S. forces," and "fuels the belief out there that Americans are anti-Islam.

John McCain made a huge understatement yesterday on CBS saying that, "the effect will probably in some areas give ISIS some more propaganda." Duh....

Mr. President, you just handed terrorists and would be terrorists a gift beyond their wildest dreams. The next time they attack us, we'll know why.

1/31/17

Hey Donald,

You've been hijacked by Steve Bannon. For all practical purposes, he is now the President. Jared Kushner, is furious. He goes away on Fridays at sundown to observe Shabbat and is gone all day Saturday. You penned your hateful anti-immigration order 16 minutes before sundown last Friday and the next day all hell broke loose. If I were Jared (or Ivanka), I'd bail. Donald, you're losing your own family - and….your Presidency. In the meantime, Mike Pence must be licking his chops.

Back to Bannon. You just promoted this brash, racist political operative to the National Security Council. Politics and national security go together like nitroglycerin and paint shakers.

This is the guy who left out any mention of Jews in the recent White House statement commemorating the Holocaust, who ran a headline referring to Bill Kristol as a "renegade Jew", who allegedly said he "didn't want 'his' daughter to attend a Los Angeles school because of the number of Jews there", who was charged in 1996 with misdemeanor domestic violence, who the Southern Poverty Law Center describes as being on the "extremist fringe", and who is supported by the KKK.

So this is your guy, huh?

2/1/17

Hey Donald,

Well, I guess it was too much to hope for. Given your penchant for drama, I thought there might be a possibility that you would surprise all of us and re-nominate Merrick Garland for SCOTUS. Can you imagine the look of horror on Mitch's McConnell's face? Garland would most likely have been confirmed unanimously. How could the Republicans not vote for him after what they did?

But your pick, Neil Gorsuch seems to be a bright guy with impressive credentials. He even scolded the Senate back in 2002 for "grossly mistreating" Merrick Garland by delaying his confirmation to the US Court of Appeals in Washington DC for 18 months. Imagine what he thought when the Senate refused to even consider Garland's nomination during Obama's presidency.

So this seat was stolen from one of the most qualified and centrist jurists of our time. I wouldn't blame the Democrats in the Senate at all for playing tit for tat, but I hope they take the high road, ask probing questions, and if no bombs are found, vote to confirm.

The balance on the court won't shift - Gorsuch apparently is a spitting image of Scalia. I wonder if he will protect free speech like Scalia did in Texas v. Johnson in 1989 - the famous flag burning case. It seems that's all we have left...for now at least.

2/2/17

Hey Donald,

Have you ever cried as an adult? Just a few weeks ago you admitted that you hadn't cried since you were a baby, but is this really true? It seems about all I ever see on your face is rage, anger and contempt.

You mocked Chuck Schumer on Monday accusing him of shedding "fake tears". Schumer was overcome with emotion while standing next to a Syrian refugee family that was detained at the airport. He called your immigration ban "mean-spirited and un-American". Your first instinct was to put him down.

It seems that you need to mock others to feel good about yourself, just as you did to Serge Kovaleski, an award-winning journalist with deformities to his hands and arms who called you out about one of your many lies. How can you be so callous?

President Obama shed tears for the victims of war and domestic terrorism many times. John Boehner could barely contain himself after Gabby Giffords returned to work after having been shot in the head by an American terrorist. This behavior is normal for anyone who feels compassion for another human being.

You also said recently that the last time you said your were sorry was "a long time ago". A certain part of me feels sorry for you.

2/3/17

Hey Donald,

The National Prayer Breakfast is supposed to be a solemn occasion, designed to bring people of faith together to celebrate their diversity, to inspire, and to do so with dignity and humility - yes, humility....

So then you prayed yesterday that Arnold Schwarzenegger (your replacement on The Apprentice) would bring ratings back up. The Terminator suggested that you switch jobs (not a bad idea), and then he mentioned your own approval ratings, which are the lowest of any incoming president in US history. Touché....

Then you said that you wanted to do away with the Johnson Amendment. This measure forbids tax exempt organizations like churches from endorsing political candidates.

Jerry Falwell Jr. runs a tax exempt school and was one of the first evangelical leaders to support you. Liberty University, which Falwell heads is worth more than a billion dollars. Many of it's students believe the Earth was created 6,000 years ago.

You just appointed this man to lead your new educational task force, where one of his main goals is to dismantle federal rules requiring schools to investigate sexual assault.

2/4/17

Hey Donald,

I've been pretty hard on you lately for doing some really stupid things, but today I want to thank you for doing something right.

According to Politico, your daughter and her husband convinced you to dump an executive order overturning Obama's initiative designed to protect LGBT rights. Those on the far right in your administration, including Mike Pence, came up with this order in hopes of furthering their insidious, hateful agenda.

These religious fascists are relentless - please stand your ground. Discrimination of any kind must not be tolerated in our society.

As Governor of Indiana, Mike Pence signed what was called the "Religious Freedom Restoration Act". The backlash was intense, and the state lost millions of dollars. They are still reeling from the impact. Had you not picked Pence as your Vice President, his political life would have been over. He knows that too.

Here's where Pence is coming from. In 2006, he said that same-sex couples were a sign of "societal collapse."

2/5/17

Hey Donald,

Up here in the Pacific Northwest, we have a lot to be proud of. We've got the Seahawks, Microsoft, Boeing, Amazon, The Bill and Melinda Gates Foundation, and now....James Robart.

You know him - he's the George Bush appointed federal judge who stopped your ill conceived immigration ban dead in it's tracks. This guy is no slacker - like Gorsuch, Robart was confirmed unanimously by the Senate for his seat on the bench.

After his ruling, you went into your dictator mode and tweeted: "The opinion of this so-called judge, which essentially takes law-enforcement away from our country, is ridiculous and will be overturned!" "So-called judge"? He IS a judge, and was appointed by a Republican like you. "Takes law enforcement away from our country"? What do you mean? He just enforced the law!

Do you and Bannon know what you are doing? I do. You guys are undermining our Democracy and attempting to sabotage our Constitution by pitting one independent branch of government against another. We've seen it before with Judge Curiel who you also slammed for challenging you in your university fraud case.

That one cost you $25 million.

2/6/17

Hey Donald,

Well, you lost in the Appeals Court with your immigration ban.

Those of us who read your tweets saw that your rage continued over the weekend. You wrote, "Just cannot believe a judge would put our country in such peril. If something happens blame him and court system. People pouring in. Bad!"

Why do you continue to bash the judiciary? This case will be decided on the merits by highly qualified deep thinkers. This is how things work in the real world. Relax!

And this, "I have instructed Homeland Security to check people coming into our country VERY CAREFULLY. The courts are making the job very difficult!" No, Donald. They are just doing THEIR job and you are not being very nice to them.

You go on, "Because the ban was lifted by a judge, many very bad and dangerous people may be pouring into our country. A terrible decision." No again. People don't simply "pour" into the U.S! These people have been vetted for up to 2 years!

Meanwhile, according to The Independent, the chance of being killed by refugee in the US are 1 in 3.6 billion.

2/7/17

Hey Donald,

By now you know that political humor comes with the job. We certainly know you watched Alec Baldwin play you because you tweeted several times about how incensed you were.

As a reminder, here's Baldwin a few weeks ago at a re-enactment of your first press conference: "I want to talk about what is really important, which is jobs, because I am going to bring back a thick stream of jobs back to this country. The biggest, strongest, steadiest stream you've ever seen. This country will be literally showered with jobs. Because I am a major wiz at jobs. It will be a golden opportunity for me as president to make a big splash."

NBC is working on a primetime edition of Saturday Night Live. You may have already heard that the SNL viewership is up 22%!

Politico reports that you had a REALLY hard time with Melissa McCarthy playing your press secretary, Sean Spicer last weekend. They said your contempt was not so much about the skit itself, but the fact that Spicer was played by a woman!

This is worrisome to me and a lot of others. Seriously....lighten up. You need to be able to take a joke. Things will get a lot worse (or funnier) before they get better.

2/8/17

Hey Donald,

Pence made history yesterday! It was the first time EVER that a VP had to break a tie vote for a cabinet nominee - in this case, Betsy DeVos, for the Education Dept. What's that say about her?

Did you watch her confirmation hearing? If so, even you might have cringed. You need guns in school to shoot grizzly bears that might walk through the door to eat the kids' lunch? Really?

Aside from her lack of qualifications, DeVos seems intent on destroying public education. Vouchers are her big thing, especially for Christian schools. While the Establishment Clause is open to interpretation, just like many people do not want their taxes used to fund abortion, for example, I do not want my tax dollars going toward any school where the theory of Creationism is taught, and the theory of Evolution is not.

So what if, someone wanted to send their kid to a Wiccan school using a voucher? Christian taxpayers would be forced to fund what they might call, "devil worship". It's not, but that's what a lot of people think. The argument goes both ways.

BTW, during her nomination hearings, Ms. DeVos didn't deny that her family had contributed over $200 million to the Republican Party over the years.

2/9/17

Hey Donald,

I hate to keep bringing up your mental state, but it's become so worrisome, I can't not share my concerns with you.

I continue to read things from really smart and experienced people, including Republicans and conservatives that are unsettling, to say the least. Here are just a few examples.

From Eliot Cohen, a senior State Dept. official under President Bush, "I've been in this town for 26 years. I have never seen anything like this. I genuinely do not think this is a mentally healthy president." From Elizabeth Rosenberg, a counterterrorism expert at the Treasury Dept. regarding your bombastic tweets, "I think it's a cry for help," and that you are motivated by, "incredulity, and the need to share it." Or legendary journalist, Carl Bernstein, saying on TV recently that your "emotional maturity and stability are being discussed in private by senior members of his own political party".

Then according to your new National Security Advisor, Michael Flynn, you called him a few days ago around 3:00 AM to ask if a strong dollar or a weak one was good for the economy. Isn't this something a President should know? There's always Google!

Oh, that's right - I forgot. You don't use a computer.

2/10/17

Hey Donald,

4 out of 4 judges have now said that your travel ban was bogus. So you took the last 3 to the cleaners (twitter) saying, "SEE YOU IN COURT". Boy you must have been fuming since you used caps this time. We're all wondering how you will react when you lose at SCOTUS. Or maybe your new AG, Jeff Sessions, will decide it's not worth it to go there because he's sure to lose. If he does, are you going to throw him under the bus too?

Looking back at where this started, it seems that an 8th grade civics student could have handled your order better, in which case you might have stood a chance.

For starters, you included green card holders, many of whom were Iranians who fled their homes in the 80's to get away from Islamic fundamentalism. Isn't that what you are trying to combat?

Then after the blowup in Seattle, you tried to save face and not admit an error (which you are incapable of), and instead of merely tweaking the order with one sentence, your lawyer essentially told the 9th Circuit that he had "authoritative guidance" to clarify that green card holders were exempt. The judges scoffed.

Finally your guy told the court that your order was "unreviewable" - in other words, get out of the way. They didn't like that either.

22

2/11/17

Hey Donald,

Either your national security advisor, Michael Flynn, or Mike Pence lied this past week, which of course is nothing new among you and your tribe. But this one is REALLY serious.

Flynn called Russian Ambassador Sergey Kislyak after the election, and 9 security officials confirmed that Flynn said that Trump would lift the sanctions that Obama placed on Russia for interfering in the election. This was illegal and the FBI is on it.

So on Wednesday, Flynn twice denied talking about sanctions, but then once more details came out, an aide said that Flynn "couldn't be certain that the topic never came up."

Here's where Pence comes in saying on CBS, "They did not discuss anything having to do with the United States' decision to expel diplomats or impose censure against Russia". He then went on to say that there had been no contact between Trump's team and Russia before the election!!! What he didn't think about was that the security apparatus monitors all calls of this nature.

Flynn was fired from his position as head of the Defense Intelligence Agency in 2014 for incompetence. His son was fired from the transition team for spreading fake news about Hillary Clinton, which lead to a shooting

2/12/17

Hey Donald,

I can see it coming. I wrote to you 10 days after your Inauguration with your "so called" record crowds and suggested that your ill conceived and illegal immigration ban instantly created thousands of new terrorists around the world who are now even more determined to attack us. They are in full retaliation mode.

They will probably hit us again at some point and when they do, I'm afraid you will change the logo on your red cap to, "I Told You So", when in fact, it should read, "I Made It Happen".

You will use this this event(s) to destroy our civil liberties by suspending Due Process, locking up free speech practitioners and immigrants (legal or not), and anyone else who challenges your faux authority.

I for one will not be cowed. Millions of us will stand up and resist in whatever way we must to ensure our survival. Dozens of Republicans in the House and Senate are squirming in private, but unfortunately they do not have the moral authority to question your behavior.

Dissent is patriotic and we will make our voices heard.

2/13/17

Hey Donald,

I wrote to you recently about your National Security Advisor, Michael Flynn violating a federal law a few weeks ago. Then last week, your spokesperson, Kellyanne Conway, broke a federal ethics rule by endorsing your daughter's clothing line on TV. I'm wondering who's next.

Your press secretary said that she was "counseled" for doing what she did, but Patricia Arquette asked in a tweet, "Who counseled her? A priest? A minister? An exorcist? Someone from Arby's? An old soda can? A lotto scratcher? Who?" She asks good questions. You might consider her for a role on your team.

So then according to the AP, you "took issue" with what Spicer said, believing that it wasn't fair to say that she got "counseled" because that sounded like she was in trouble.

Well, she WAS in trouble - she broke the law. Even the House Oversight Committee chairman, Jason Chaffetz rebuked her.

In case you hadn't noticed, she wants to be your chief of staff and is pulling as many strings as she can to get the job. She tweeted after the blow up, "POTUS supports me, and millions of Americans support him and his agenda".

2/14/17

Hey Donald,

Have a heart. Civil Asset Forfeiture is one of the most heinous and diabolical practices in the US and it occurs daily. Essentially it means that a law enforcement officer can confiscate cash, arms, cars, you name it, as soon as they accuse the victim of committing a crime. The stolen goods do not even have to relate to that so-called crime! They can steal with no accountability.

So last week you met with representatives of the National Sheriff's Association, and one of the attendees told you, "we've got a state senator in Texas that was talking about introducing legislation to require conviction before we could receive that forfeiture money." "Can you believe that?" you cried!

Then you asked for the person's name so you could "destroy his career". The sheriffs howled. If this was a joke like somebody from your camp told CNN, it was a really dumb one.

According to the Institute for Justice, around $29 billion in cash and goods has been seized between 2001 and 2014 with no judicial review. Many were innocent of any wrongdoing and were never convicted of a crime.

Your new AG, Jeff Sessions is a big fan of this practice.

2/15/17

Hey Donald,

You've been in office less than a month and already you are facing a crisis that pales in comparison to Watergate. Do you remember the question back then, "what did the President know and when did he know it?"

Apparently your team had repeated contacts with the Russians before you were elected, and then there were the infamous calls between Michael Flynn and the Russian ambassador colluding over reducing sanctions that were imposed because they helped you win. Spicer said that you fired Flynn because you lost confidence in him.

No, you fired him because the story broke. It appears that he may have committed a felonious act, and may have to testify under oath. I'm wondering if he will throw you under the bus....

If you would have dumped Flynn when you first heard about the calls there wouldn't be rumblings of a cover-up, which brought down Nixon. You seem real intent on being close buddies with Russia - is it because of your business interests over there?

BTW, Putin just deployed a cruise missile in violation of a 1987 treaty that bans intermediate-range missiles. What's the plan?

2/16/17

Hey Donald,

I read this recently in a piece by Richard Cohen from the Washington Post. He's far more articulate than me, so I thought I would copy the following paragraph and send it to you. Perhaps you have read it, but I doubt it. It's too good not to pass along.

"Trump is a particularly bad role model for our children. A father instructs. He raises a child to be good, to be honest, to tell the truth, to be humble, to be fair, not to be petty, to respect women, to accept fair criticism, to protect the weak and not to injure the injured, such as the bereaved parents of a son who died heroically in Iraq and a reporter with a physical disability. Trump teaches otherwise. He shows a boy that the manly virtues are for suckers, that the narcissism of youth should be cherished and that angry impulses have to be honored. Lots of men have failed as presidents, as Trump surely will, but few fail so dismally as role models. He's a boy's idea of a man. He's a man's idea of a boy."

You may want to consider this the next time you feel like lashing out on Twitter. You don't always have to be right. You do not need to be vindictive. Grace, kindness, tolerance, and goodness are virtues, which you seem incapable of showing.

2/17/17

Hey Donald,

As a patriotic American, I am seriously embarrassed - and afraid. Your news conference yesterday was appalling. I have closely watched politics for over 40 years and have never seen this kind of indignant ranting, institution bashing, atrocious vitriol, horrific lying, and reprehensible demeanor coming from a "so-called" leader of the free world. Even Fox News was appalled.

You've been stewing in a poisonous cauldron of your own making for a month, and now you are unleashing your juvenile fury on everything around you, blaming everyone but yourself. Your approval ratings are tanking precariously and it's not the fault of news organizations. It's your fault. Period.

Now you're going to Florida to hold a rally. As before, your "adoring" crowd will be made up of largely gullible, uninformed, angry white people whom you will whip into a raging frenzy, all the while boasting about yourself. This seems to fill your tortured soul with faux approval that you obviously never received from your father as a child. You have deceived your base and they will soon discover the truth. The campaign is over and it's time for reality.

You are unfit for the office you hold. I'm sorry, but you did not inherit a mess. Sadly, it's your own Presidency that's a mess.

2/18/17

Hey Donald

Melissa Blake wrote a heart rendering article in the NYT on Monday. She's a journalist, physically disabled, and wrote that she's never been more scared.

She went to The White House website recently and discovered that the disabilities section had been deleted. I just did a search myself and found that a search for "Americans With Disabilities Act" produced no results. Whoever did this in your administration is callous and cruel, but sadly they were merely taking your lead. Everyone in the country remembers your mocking of a disabled man, which essentially gave license to others with no empathy to do the same.

For the benefit of the doubt assume they are doing some updates. Couldn't the existing information have been left intact for people like Ms. Blake to access in the meantime? Before you assumed office, a paragraph from the Disabilities page read, "The President is committed to nurturing a society that values the contributions of all of our citizens and residents, including the approximately 50 million people in this country living with disabilities."

How do you think Melissa and many other disabled people felt when the page representing them turned up missing?

2/19/17

Hey Donald

There has been way too much talk about your hair on the news - it's really petty and insignificant. However, it appears that your mane may be a national security issue. Let me explain.

Your long time personal physician, Dr. Harold N. Bornstein let slip a few weeks ago that you are taking a drug called finasteride, which is used to treat male-pattern baldness. This wasn't disclosed in a letter that Bornstein wrote in 5 minutes in December of 2015 regarding your health. He also made the preposterous claim that, "If elected, Mr. Trump, I can state unequivocally, will be the healthiest individual ever elected to the Presidency". I wonder how he knew that since most previous Presidents are dead.

So according to The Men's Journal, major side effects of finasteride are the possibility of confusion, chronic depression, insomnia, brain fog, and suicidal thoughts. The FDA is questioning this drug's safety as a result of more than 1,200 lawsuits having been filed against Merck (the maker) since 2011.

So what if another guy with an interesting hairdo (Kim Jong-un from North Korea) launches a missile at us and you are experiencing brain fog?

2/20/17

Hey Donald,

Congressional Republicans are now having to face the music. It's ear piercing, pounding, and getting louder. I've never seen them squirm more in my life. After years of dissing Obamacare, trying 62 times to repeal the law, and wasting millions of our tax dollars trying, the chickens have come home to roost.

According to the bipartisan Committee for a Responsible Federal Budget, a full repeal of Obamacare would cost $350 billion. AND, according to The Commonwealth Fund, up to 3 million jobs in the health industry and other associated areas would disappear. On top of that, up to $1.5 trillion would be lost in gross state product in the coming years. We can hear the gulping thousands of miles away.

You guys keep saying you are going to replace The Affordable Care Act with something cheaper and better. How? The Republicans had 7 years to do so, but they didn't because nothing better exists without allowing people to die with no coverage like they did before the Act.

Obama haters hate the mandate, but everyone keeps forgetting that this was a Republican idea originating at The Heritage Foundation, a Republican think tank. It was the basis for Mitt Romney's health care program in Massachusetts when he was governor.

2/21/17

Hey Donald,

You have lost the most important thing most fundamental to your success - credibility. No one except your clueless supporters believe you anymore. Even Mitch McConnell says he "has no idea" when asked about one of your lies.

The nonexistent Swedish terror incident you mentioned in Florida on Saturday is the latest, but let's not forget about your inauguration crowd size (way smaller than you keep saying), your standing ovation at the CIA (they were already standing), the millions of illegal votes (none of the 50 state secretaries have confirmed this), the increase in the murder rate (it's declining), winning the most electoral votes since Reagan (completely false), and the list goes on and on and on. You even lied under oath 30 times in December of 2007 during a deposition after you sued Timothy L. O'Brien regarding a book he wrote. You lost the case.

During your campaign, you called Hillary Clinton a "pathological liar". Washington Post's Fact Checker awarded you 4 Pinocchios (the maximum number a statement can receive) 59 times. During that same period, Clinton earned 7.

This may be your Achilles Heel. "I have nothing to do with Russia. To the best of my knowledge, no person that I deal with does." Only trouble is, your people's calls to Russia were monitored.

2/22/17

Hey Donald,

You campaigned incessantly on rebuilding our infrastructure, but you only got around to releasing a (very flawed) proposal 2 weeks before your election. You told us that you were going to immediately hire thousands of people to rebuild roads, bridges, airports, etc. However, you forgot about something.

In an interview in December, you told the New York Times that you hadn't realized that spending a huge amount of money on this effort would alienate conservatives. "That's not a very Republican thing to do - I didn't even know that, frankly", you said. Huh? Paul Ryan and Mitch McConnell are virtually silent on this issue.

On the other hand, Obama and his team spent months during his campaign 8 years ago hammering out a thorough infrastructure plan, and 4 weeks after his inauguration, with congressional approval, signed the Recovery Act which included $98 billion in infrastructure spending. He did his homework and it helped save our economy, which was in free fall at the time.

It's clear why you have gotten very little done in the first few weeks of your administration in comparison to past presidents. You have no patience for the slow grind of politics or the willingness to study and grasp fundamental policy details. In a nutshell, you are lazy, except when it comes to self promotion.

2/23/17

Hey Donald,

Some of your strongest supporters who voted for you were farmers from California's Central Valley. They didn't think you were serious about deporting their help, but now they are worried sick. It's tempting to say, "I told you so".

It appears that the roundup of undocumented field and dairy workers is about to begin. Do your sons Eric and Donald Jr. know how to milk cows or pick lettuce? They may be needed to help keep the farms out there afloat.

70% of US fieldworkers are here illegally. California alone is responsible for $35 billion worth of farm production each year. If this industry were to collapse, food prices and unemployment would skyrocket, with economic disaster rippling across the state.

If you think that immigrants are taking these jobs away from hard working Americans, think again.

In 2011, Alabama passed HB 56, the harshest state immigration law in the country. Illegals fled the state by the thousands and the program turned into a colossal train wreck. Crops rotted in the fields and the state economy trembled. Right wing politicians who pushed the law through out of hatred and spite backtracked from political pressure and the law is now in shambles.

2/24/17

Hey Donald,

Yesterday you rescinded federal guidelines allowing transgender students to use the bathroom that conformed to their gender identity. Your new Education Secretary, Betsy DeVos was not a happy camper. Interestingly enough, she is a strong supporter of gay marriage as well as the rights of the LGBT community.

Even though during your campaign you supported the rights of transgender people to "use the bathroom they feel is appropriate", you caved in to your off-the-charts right wing Attorney General, Jeff Sessions. He went to you after he couldn't get DeVos to relent, since she had to sign off on the measure too. She either had to get on board or resign. She caved then too. Once again this shows that you have few strong convictions.

Did you not read about the turmoil that North Carolina and Indiana created when they passed discriminating laws? These states lost millions of dollars as no respectable business wants to be associated with discrimination. Our country will be divided now more than ever as each state develops it's own policy.

OK, so what if a little girl is in the restroom by herself and a big, hulking transgender man with short hair, a beard, piercings, tattoos, and heavy black combat boots walks in with his chains jingling. Don't you think that little girl might feel a bit threatened?

2/25/17

Hey Donald,

You and your groupies are about to write a new "trickle down" tax code, with the idea that if taxes are cut on the rich, the economy benefits and everybody wins. It ain't gonna happen - never has, never will. Even Reagan's budget director, David Stockman, who rebranded trickle down as "Reaganomics", later disparaged the idea. The International Monetary Fund in 2015 also said it doesn't work. You guys just end up hoarding the money.

Take a look at Kansas. In 2011 when Sam Brownback was elected Governor, he dumped the top income tax bracket and then figured out a way to allow thousands of business owners to pay no income taxes at all, including Koch Industries subsidiaries.

It backfired. The budget is decimated, economic growth stagnated, and job growth is dead. Soon they will be $500 million short to fund even basic services. The Republican Legislature just passed a bill that would raise around $1 billion and eliminate most of the cuts. Brownback plans to veto the measure.

So why then do you and they keep pushing this idea? The answer is simple. You cut taxes on the rich, they in turn finance your political campaigns, and then you get elected.

Yes indeed, we have the best politicians money can buy.

2/26/17

Hey Donald,

You are the luckiest man in politics....for now.
Imagine if just one of the legislative bodies was
controlled by Democrats, I seriously believe your
presidency would be very short lived. Here's why.

Republicans are planning to dump a rare Democratic
"resolution of inquiry" next week that would have
forced the disclosure of your ties to Russia. We know
you have them. Your son-in-law, Jared, said you did.
Flynn's phone calls to Russia prove it.

So instead of facing an embarrassing vote on the
floor, and showing the entire nation that they are
covering up for you, the Republican leadership came
up with an obscure rule that allows them to send the
resolution to the House Judiciary Committee first
where it will certainly die.

The Republican controlled committee then plans to
vote on the resolution the same day that you address
Congress, meaning that it will be buried in the news
cycle.

This resolution could have forced you and your
Attorney General to give up "any document, record,
memo, correspondence, or other communication"
pertaining to "criminal or counterintelligence
investigations" related to you, your staff, or your
business. You are close to being outed.

2/27/17

Hey Donald,

Do you ever listen to the radio? Or more specifically, NPR? I understand that you get most all of your news and information from Fox and other "fake" cable news channels. I don't think you have the intellectual curiosity to listen to anything else.

Word has it that you are planning to axe The National Endowment for the Arts and Humanities, which partially funds NPR and PBS and to rub salt into the wound, you want to privatize the Corporation for Public Broadcasting. Shame on you.

Federal funding for these arts programs is a mere 0.0625% of the budget. Reagan tried to de-fund these programs and was met with so much hostility, he backed down. Many Republicans joined in this effort to maintain these valuable institutions. As a 40 year listener to NPR, I will fight hard on this one.

It seems that you want to make these cuts as examples of taxpayer waste.

I have a better example. Take fewer trips to Mar-a-Lago, which are costing us taxpayers $3 million a trip. Then kick back on the White House lawn with your kid and listen to "The TED Radio Hour". You may just learn something new.

2/28/17

Hey Donald,

Do you remember John Dean? He's the guy who testified against your idol Richard Nixon, who was kicked out of office. On Friday, Dean said that your first month has "echoes of Watergate". I couldn't agree more.

Last week after the FBI refused to do so, your people called several other intelligence agencies and asked them to tamp down stories in the media about your ties to Russia.

Do you know what this is called? It's an attempted COVER UP. It's becoming more and more obvious that you have something to hide, given your hatred and disdain for the media, Yes, journalists - the same ones who brought you fame and fortune....and the same ones who helped you get elected.

Here's the irony. Supposedly you have a framed letter to you from Richard Nixon hanging in your office. It reads "Dear Donald, I did not see the program but Mrs. Nixon told me that you were great on 'The Donahue Show'. "As you can imagine, she is an expert on politics and she predicts that whenever you decide to run for office you will be a winner!"

Well Pat was right - you did win. But it also looks like you may be on the same road to losing it all, just like Dick.

3/1/17

Hey Donald,

You were a fine showman last night - something you have gotten good at over the years as a TV star. However I wasn't impressed. Putting aside the blatant falsehoods (there were many), it was what you did earlier in the day that got to me.

Ordinarily you like to sign things with a lot of smiling people standing around and shaking your hand - you know, the kind of adulation that you thrive on. This time you didn't because you knew you'd be called out, AND you did it on the same day as your speech, making sure the story would get buried.

The rule you signed into law rolls back one of President Obama's important regulations, which made it harder for mentally ill people to buy guns. These are people who have been deemed unfit to even handle their own affairs! So now, around 75,000 people with marginal mental aptitude can go out and legally buy guns.

This was nothing but a great big chunk of red meat that you threw out to the NRA, who are among your most vocal supporters. Where's the logic in this action other than spite? It makes no sense at all.

Adam Lanza who killed 20 first graders at Sandy Hook Elementary School in 2013 suffered from Asperger's Syndrome and possible schizophrenia.

3/2/17

Hey Donald,

As Commander in Chief, you botched your first big military operation and then you had the audacity to blame your generals for losing a man, rather than taking full responsibility yourself as all previous presidents have done. The buck stops in your office.

Just hours before delivering your speech yesterday in which you rightly honored fallen Navy Seal, Ryan Owens, you said on Fox, "This was a mission that was started before I got here. This was something that was, just — they wanted to do. And they came to me, and they explained what they wanted to do — the generals — who are very respected, and they lost Ryan".

You seemed to shift the blame to Obama again, who never fully signed off on the raid. His administration got you up to speed assuming you would do your own homework, which you obviously didn't. Everything that could go wrong, went wrong, including the death of multiple women and children and the loss of a $75 million Osprey. John McCain called the mission a failure. Multiple sources told NBC that no actionable intelligence was obtained.

According to Sean Spicer, you were up in your residence during the raid. A tweet went out from your account shortly after the shooting began, announcing your upcoming TV appearance on the Christian Broadcasting Network.

3/3/17

Hey Donald,

So your new Attorney General, Jeff Sessions goes to Congress and testifies that he never had any contacts with the Russian government during your campaign. When Al Franken asked him in January under oath what he might do if he found out that anyone working on your campaign had talked to the Russian government, Sessions said, "I'm not aware of any of those activities" and "I did not have communications with the Russians." Sessions was your foreign policy advisor then.

There's more. In response to Senator Leahy's written question to Sessions, "Have you been in contact with anyone connected to any part of the Russian government about the 2016 election, either before or after election day?", Sessions answered, "No".

He spoke twice with Russia's ambassador to the US, Sergey Kislyak. One of those meetings occurred during the Russia's interference in the presidential race. The subject had to have come up - it was some of the biggest news at the time.

Sessions finally recused himself, but that's not enough. You fired Michael Flynn for misleading Mike Pence about his contacts with Russia. Misleading the Senate under oath is far more serious. You must also fire Jeff Sessions. If you don't, one could argue that you see him as one of your last bulwarks against your own indictment for colluding with the Russians.

3/4/17

Hey Donald,

In 2008, you bought a house in Palm Beach for $40 million. The locals said it was gaudy and full of fake art and mold. It sat empty for 2 years before you finally sold it to a Russian oligarch, Dmitry Rybolovlev for $100 million. He never moved in.

Apparently you really needed money at the time to pay off some loans, so this sale with a $60 million profit came just at the right time. Rybolovlev was buying anything he could get his hands on as he was desperately trying to park his money anywhere he could find so his ex-wife couldn't get it.

OK, so the Deutsche Bank was recently fined $630 million for laundering billions of dollars in Russian money. You were a bad risk because you were so far in debt, but Deutsche apparently loaned you more than a billion dollars anyway even though they were struggling. Deutsche was funneling money through the Bank of Cypress, which is part owned by Rybolovlev, who paid way too much for a house that's now being torn down.

Oh, Wilbur Ross, your new Commerce Secretary and an old friend of yours, was Vice Chairman of the Bank of Cypress before he got his new job. Presumably he introduced you to your fancy Russian home buyer. Was Ross' job your payoff to him for enabling you to come up with such a sweet deal?

3/5/17

Hey Donald,

Your twitter rant yesterday morning was epic. You accused Obama of wiretapping your phones with absolutely no proof whatsoever. Your aides say you were livid to begin with - not over Sessions' lying under oath, but because he recused himself from any investigations regarding your Russian connections.

You wanted to continue to glow in the aftermath of your successful speech on Tuesday night, but instead you melted down and let loose. According to CNN, "Nobody has seen him that upset. The President's mood is adding to tremendous pressure inside the West Wing and aides have been seen in tears in recent days at multiple meetings."

Congressman Ted Lieu's tweet sums it up, "Mr. President: If there was a wiretap at Trump Tower, that means a fed judge found probable cause of crime which means you are in deep shit."

It's extremely unlikely that you were wiretapped. All we can surmise is that you feel cornered and are panicking. The evidence is closing in around you through multiple investigations.

And then, as of that weren't enough, in your last tweet you accused Arnold Schwarzenegger of getting fired for bad ratings on your TV show, The Apprentice.

3/6/17

Hey Donald,

One of the biggest mysteries so far has to do with Melania's declaration on November 3rd that as First Lady, she planned to work to combat bullying if you got elected. A lot of people are wondering if this was a not-so-subtle cry for help. She said:

"We have to find a better way to talk to each other, to disagree with each other, to respect each other. We must find better ways to honor and support the basic goodness of our children, especially in social media. It will be one of the main focuses of my work if I'm privileged enough to become your first lady."

Do you think your tweets have met your wife's criteria?

You have essentially given permission to a vast number of people to bully others by your behavior. The numbers indisputably show an uptick in attacks of minorities, the Jewish community, the LGBT community, etc.

No one who works in the anti-bullying field has yet heard from Melania, including Sameer Hinduja, the co-director of the Cyberbullying Research Center at Florida Atlantic University.

Did you stop her in her tracks because you realized that some of us might make a connection?

3/7/17

Hey Donald,

At the risk of belaboring this issue, you obviously didn't think things through before you went on your twitter tirade on Saturday. Usually someone in your position bounces things off others, who may perhaps be a little smarter, before making such bold claims.

Your inability to control your temper, even when it's against your own interests, is the most worrisome thing facing our nation.

Regardless of your motives - extreme paranoia, an effort to distract the media from ongoing Russian probes, etc., you've placed yourself into a no win situation.

Let's say that Congress does go ahead and open an inquiry. They would have to start with the question of why was a wiretap ordered on you in the first place. This will inevitably hasten the conclusion that you and your accomplices were complicit in the Russian government's meddling of our elections. Did you not think about that?

But what if the Republicans deny your request for a hearing? None of them have supported your claim. Even the FBI Director has repudiated your notion and has suggested that the Justice Department do the same. Did you not think about how embarrassing this public rebuke would be? Given your nature, I hope this doesn't cause you to do something really stupid.

3/8/17

Hey Donald,

Health insurance is at the top of the news since the Republicans came out with their plan to replace The Affordable Care Act. You promised during the campaign that everyone had to be covered and by all accounts, this plan does not fulfill that promise. It appears that it will be far more expensive than Obamacare and will cover fewer people.

According to CNN Money, repealing and replacing Obamacare will give a tax windfall to the richest people in the country while at the same time will increase the taxes of those making $10 - $75 thousand per year. Robert Reich, the former Secretary of Labor, claims that people like you will get a $7 million tax break out of the deal. Is this really the road you want to go down?

So why has the mandate (originally a Republican idea) become so evil? Why isn't the requirement to have auto insurance just as evil? Isn't the idea to spread the risk and keep premiums low? Who will pay for the care of those who will not buy insurance and who have an accident or get really sick? Taxpayers, of course.

You and the Republicans have made the word, "Obamacare" toxic to get elected. The program was sound - it just needed tweaking. I hope that people don't end up dying again for lack of affordable care.

3/9/17

Hey Donald,

Somehow the religious right is enamored with you. I don't get it. You admitted to being a sexual predator on camera, you've bullied your way through life while rarely apologizing or admitting a mistake, you've lied more times than anyone can count, you've stiffed multiple contractors over the years, you supported abortion rights until you began your campaign for the presidency, you're twice divorced, and you seem to care about no one but yourself.

I have a number of Christian friends and some are the finest people I know. Most of these friends are repulsed by your behavior - and now your policy decisions. Jesus would certainly not have supported you like the 66% of evangelicals do. They are either "fake Christians for profit" or are completely clueless and are not yet aware of what's about to hit them.

The rich Jesus people are salivating over the tax breaks that they are about to get with your new health insurance law, and don't seem to care about the millions of people who will be priced out of the health insurance market, many of whom will die as a result. When Paul Ryan was asked about these tax breaks, he laughed.

On a larger scale, it seems that many of these so-called Christians are hunkering down for a religious war against immigrants, the Muslim faith, the poor - and you seem to be a pawn in their insidious game.

2/10/17

Hey Donald,

Your recent appointment adds to the intrigue - you chose a fellow billionaire, Jon Huntsman, to be the new ambassador to Russia.

Huntsman dissed you repeatedly during the campaign. You did the same to him in a series of tweets when he was ambassador to China, saying, "China did a major number on us during the reign of Jon Huntsman. He was easy pickins." You have a history of holding a grudge against anyone who ever crosses you, so this makes your appointment even more curious.

Huntsman is "craven and opportunistic" according to the WA Post. In 2009, he wrote to Obama, "you are a remarkable leader – and it has been a great honor getting to know you", and then he proceeded to launch his campaign for president while still an ambassador! After you admitted groping women, he said he would never meet with you, assuming your campaign was over.

Then you got elected and Huntsman flipped. His love fest for you began and hasn't stopped. He even supported you calling Taiwan after the election even though he knew it was a serious breach.

So given Huntsman's apparent malleability, are you going to use him to cover up your conspiracy with the Russians to sabotage our electoral process?

3/11/17

Hey Donald,

Here's something you should think about. Next month, Arkansas will execute 8 prisoners, which is a third of the number of those who were killed in all states by the government in 2016.

Why? Because Arkansas' stash of death drugs is about to expire. They use Midazolam for these killings, which is supposed to bring on a more relaxed death, when in fact, this same drug has been the cause of multiple botched executions in the past. As Supreme court Sonia Sotomayor said in 2015, being injected with this drug is "the chemical equivalent of being burned at the stake".

A lot of drug manufacturers have been sued so they have stopped pedaling their death drugs to states. As a result, they are getting harder and harder to get.

The governor of Arkansas, Asa Hutchinson, is essentially going on a killing spree based on a date on the bottle. So why don't they change their laws and shoot prisoners instead? The subject is too squeamish for most Americans - they prefer to get their retribution "medically" rather than splattering blood around.

Donald, use your "bully" pulpit in a good way for a change. Work to end the death penalty now.

3/12/17

Hey Donald,

Sarah Palin's prediction about death panels is finally coming true. They didn't happen with Obamacare, but it appears they are about to happen under your new health care plan that's taking shape. The biggest death panel will now consist almost entirely of Republicans, and you will be chairman of the board.

The Robert Wood Johnson Foundation estimates that 24 million people will lose coverage under your new health plan by 2021.

Here's what's shocking. 45,000 people without health insurance die each year (or 1 every 12 minutes) according to The American Journal of Public Health. Studies conducted at Harvard Medical School and at Cambridge Health Alliance found that working age Americans who are uninsured are 40% more likely to die than those who have insurance.

As late as January 17th you said, "We're going to have insurance for everybody. There was a philosophy in some circles that if you can't pay for it, you don't get it. That's not going to happen with us."

So there you have it. Democrats have already picked this as their defining issue for the midterms. You guys have a choice. Come up with something that provides better and more affordable insurance for EVERYBODY and you win. Anything other than that, your party loses.

3/13/17

Hey Donald,

Almost 50 years ago, Nixon created the Environmental Protection Agency, one of his greatest achievements. Since then it has been instrumental in cleaning up our water, air, and land for those of us who live here on Planet Earth, including you.

So you picked a guy to head the EPA who has sued the agency 13 times while attorney general of Oklahoma in an effort to roll back regulations. Then in a fit of delusion last week he said that carbon dioxide did not contribute to climate change in any meaningful way. Practically every scientist in the world disagrees.

OK so there's a legal opinion in place called an "endangerment finding" that says that large amounts of carbon dioxide harms human health. The Supreme Court confirmed that the gas met the definition of a pollutant under the Clean Air Act.

There's talk now that you plan to issue another order directing Pruitt to start ripping apart this endangerment finding pertaining to power plant emissions - in other words, allow more carbon dioxide into the atmosphere, thereby hastening global warming with catastrophic consequences.

I cry for my grandchildren sometimes because of what they face as a result of your inhumanity.

3/14/17

Hey Donald,

2 years ago, your Health and Human Services Secretary, Tom Price said this about the new CBO Director:

"Keith Hall will bring an impressive level of economic expertise and experience to the Congressional Budget Office....he has served in both the public and private sector, under presidents of both parties, and in roles that make him well-suited to lead the CBO....during his time at the U.S. International Trade Commission, Dr. Hall has worked on providing Congress with non-partisan economic analyses....his vast understanding of economic and labor market policy will be invaluable to the work of CBO and the important roll it will continue to play."

The CBO said yesterday that 24 million people would lose their health insurance under your new plan and prices for older Americans could go up as much as 700%.

You guys knew it was coming, so your tactic? Blast the CBO for incompetence. Price said yesterday that he "strenuously" disagreed with Keith Hall's assessment - the same guy he lavished praise on just 2 years earlier.

Paul Ryan, the loathsome Speaker of the House, called the bill an "act of mercy".

3/15/17

Hey Donald,

I finally realized why you want to build a wall on the Mexican border. It's not about security, it's about yourself! It all makes sense now.

Just recently you had the bid solicitation documents revised to say that "esthetics" would play a big part in who got the job to build your wall. This wall will be a monument to you, just like the Viet Nam Memorial Wall is for veterans! How many times have you said that the wall is going to be "beautiful"! I wonder how much more it will cost to make it look good. Will you insist that the lighting be chandeliers?

You keep saying the Mexicans are going to pay for the wall. They won't and we all know it. If this thing ever does get built, which is highly doubtful, it will get paid for in one of 2 ways.

The first is that you will charge the Mexicans to import their goods, which makes their products more expensive, and which ordinary Americans will then have to absorb. A hidden import tax, right?

The second is that, according to the WA Post, you would raid the budgets of the Coast Guard, the Transportation Security Agency, and the Federal Emergency Management Agency! So you take way their funding, which means more people will likely come to the US illegally.

3/16/17

Hey Donald,

You have the opportunity to go down in history as one of the most consequential presidents in modern history. Well, you already are, but for very dubious reasons.

You will never win on this health care battle. Breitbart is sabotaging Paul Ryan along with the Freedom Caucus for trying to please everybody. So then Ryan fails and you blame him. Then he loses his job, Obamacare stays in place, and you look like a schmuck, since getting rid of it was one of your biggest campaign promises. And then you blame the Democrats.

Or let's say you and Ryan ram this thing down the throats of the poor while enriching the rich even further, they finally catch on that they've been conned, and then you lose your job in 4 years.

So what can you do to make history and maybe even keep your job? After all you promised cheaper insurance for everybody.

Ditch the entire health care debate going on, reverse course, and expand Medicare for ALL. George McGovern recommended this years ago. It's simple - the infrastructure is there. Just hire a few more people to take care of the load, and then levy a few pennies for each wall street transaction to pay for it.

3/17/17

Hey Donald,

"Evil" is too kind of a word to describe your administration. The budget proposal you released yesterday is cruel and heartless.

You want to cut one of the funds that supports Meals On Wheels, which served 2.5 million low income seniors in 2015. Many old people will starve without this assistance.

You want to eliminate the grant that provides funding for poor college students. A recent study found that 14% of community college students are homeless and 2/3 don't have enough to eat.

You want to cut heating assistance for low income people forcing people to choose between eating and staying warm. 30% of young children in Boston lose weight during the winter months.

You want to cut after school and summer programs for kids in low income communities. These programs often provide nutritional meals, especially in the summertime when there's no school.

You want to cut nutrition for pregnant and nursing women which will result in more children with physical and mental impairment.

Your new budget director, Mick Mulvaney, had the audacity to call your budget "fairly compassionate".

3/18/17

Hey Donald,

Here's how twisted and diabolical things really are in your orbit.

Joseph Swedish, the head of Anthem Insurance, is pretending to like you and you fell for it as usual. It's always been the way - because of your insecurities, if someone likes you, you like them.

2 years ago Anthem wanted to take over a rival insurance company, Cigna for $48 billion....against Cigna's will. Obama's justice department filed suit because insurance rates were certain to go up, and just last month a federal judge stopped the merger.

OK, so most of the groups representing nurses, doctors, hospitals, retired people, patients, and even some insurance companies, don't like your new health care bill. Anthem, however says that they do - not because of what's in it, but for an entirely different reason.

Anthem wrote a letter to Congress supporting the health care bill primarily in an effort to get you to reverse the merger decision so they can take over Cigna. You met with Swedish in your office thinking he supported your bill, when all he wants is the merger.

Kellyanne Conway tweeted, "Progress on repeal & replace: Major insurer supportive."

3/19/17

Hey Donald,

You came out against abortion once you decided to run for president after having been pro choice for many years, which shows how disingenuous you are, but that's another matter.

Are you aware that your new health care law will result in far more abortions than are now being performed, especially if funding for Planned Parenthood is eliminated? Yes, that's right.

You want to cut Medicaid, which will result in less funding for contraceptive coverage, which will in turn increase the demand for abortions. Logic alone, and research backs this up, says that when low cost contraception is available, the abortion rate decreases. Obamacare, the health care law you and most other conservatives despised, resulted in a 14% decline in abortions between 2011 and 2014 alone.

Then to make matters worse, Congress wants to eliminate sex education in schools, again which research shows, will result in more teen pregnancies....and more abortions.

Texas slashed it's funding for family planning by 2/3 in 2011. 2 years later Medicaid costs soared, and the abortion rate increased dramatically, because of more unintended pregnancies. They were faced with reality and had to refund their programs.

3/20/17

Hey Donald,

You seem to be fond of the word "stupid".

In 2016 you said, "The world is laughing at us. They're laughing at the stupidity of our president."

During one of the debates last fall, you asked, "how stupid is our country"?

While campaigning in Iowa you asked, "how stupid are the people if Iowa"?

You said this about our leaders, "they make stupid deals, they make stupid military decisions, stupid laws".

In 2015 you said, "I know words, I have the best words. I have the best, but there is no better word than stupid."

So in the recent opinions of 2 separate Federal courts regarding your Muslim ban, the judges based their opinions in part on your own words, bolstering the charge that it was a religious test. If you would have kept your comments to yourself you might have had a chance to win your case.

How stupid was that?

3/21/17

Hey Donald,

We know you love polls. That's all you talked about during your campaign. You gushed about your lead endlessly on Twitter.

So how is that poll thing working out for you now? Not so good....

GenForward in association with the AP found in a recent poll that 57% of young adults see your presidency as illegitimate, including vast majorities of Blacks, Latinos and Asians.

They also found that only 22% of young adults think you are doing a good job and 62% think you are blowing it.

So let's look at things in general. Gallup found a few days ago that your DISAPPROVAL rating is now at 58%, which is higher than that of any rating Obama got during his entire presidency. Only 37% (your hard core base) approve of what you are doing.

To add insult to injury, your disapproval rating on Inauguration Day was almost double that of any of the last 10 presidents!

Usually new presidents experience what's called a "honeymoon" during their first 100 days, where their polls are generally high. You had trouble getting it up with the American people on your first night.

3/22/17

Hey Donald,

I feel sorry for your Press Secretary, Sean Spicer. It's sad mostly - watching someone sell his soul to the devil....

He knows when he's out there with all those reporters that there's only one person listening who matters, and that's you. Apparently you watch him with squinted eyes (just guessing), and then you dress him down afterward if you think he blew it. You even told him his suit didn't fit after his initial debut (like I would talk). Poor guy must be a nervous wreck.

Last week he was out there trying to explain your tweet rant over Obama wiretapping you. First he said he would let your tweet "speak for itself." Then later he said "wiretapping" meant something else, and dove into a very convoluted word salad.

Monday during FBI Director James Comey's hearing, Spicer said that Paul Manafort "played a very limited role for a very limited amount of time" during your campaign. What do you mean? He was your manager for 4 months, and a very influential one at that!

I'm wondering when Spicer will throw up his hands and quit - or maybe you'll fire him first. Either way I hope he describes in the book he writes about how his job was like shoveling manure for 12 hours straight in 120 degree weather with no water.

3/23/17

Hey Donald,

Gary Larson drew a cartoon once with a line of cows heading into the door of a slaughterhouse. One cow tried to get ahead of the others, which prompted another one to bellow, "Hey no cutting in line!" They apparently didn't see the sign above the door.

That's what I thought of when I saw the crowd at your speech in Louisville, KY on Monday night. They roared with approval when you told them their coal mining jobs were coming back. They're not. And besides, you're taking away their Obamacare.

Just a few hours before your speech, executives at Ohio's Dayton Power & Light announced they were going to close 2 of their coal plants this summer. They said, "without significant changes in market conditions, these plants will not be economically viable beyond mid-2018."

Global and domestic demand for coal has dropped sharply. Natural gas is generating more power than coal now and the trend continues. Gas is simply cheaper nowadays and no one in their right mind would re-open a coal mine and lose money.

You may want to consider an exit strategy when Kentucky's coal miners discover the truth.

3/24/17

Hey Donald,

If you were the father of a handicapped child, you might have thought twice about picking Neil Gorsuch for the Supreme Court. But probably not given your scorn for the disabled.

During Gorsuch's second day of testimony, all 8 Supreme Court justices slapped him down saying that he was wrong on a major disability decision he made as a judge. Talk about bad timing….

The Individuals with Disabilities Education Act (IDEA) requires that any school that accepts public funding is required to provide "free appropriate public education" to disabled students.

Chief Justice John Roberts wrote, "A focus on the particular child is at the core of the IDEA. The instruction offered must be 'specially designed' to meet a child's 'unique needs' through an individualized education program."

Gorsuch ruled against the parents of an autistic student who were seeking reimbursement for tuition they were paying at a private school that could better serve their child's needs. The school district did very little to support disabled students.

A number of legal scholars say that Gorsuch is far to the right of Clarence Thomas, now the most conservative member of the Supreme Court.

3/25/17

Hey Donald,

In your book, "The Art of the Deal", you wrote, "We must have universal health care." And then you went on:

"Just imagine the improved quality of life for our society as a whole if the issue of access to healthcare were dealt with imaginatively. With more than 40 million Americans living day to day in the fear that an illness or injury will wipe out their savings or drag them into bankruptcy, how can we truly engage in the 'pursuit of happiness' as our Founders intended."

Those words are powerful, but are now as hollow as a bell without a ringer. Why didn't you follow your own advice and approach health care imaginatively? Being imaginative might have involved improving the existing system rather than starting over. You didn't even call on the Democrats and ask for help. Instead you are now blaming them for your own failure, which is how you operate.

By going it alone, your party ended up in a circular firing squad. You could have let the Freedom Caucus stew in their own crack pot, but in the end they brought you down. Now it seems you are eager to let the system "explode" as your rage consumes you. There is no deal now, and there was certainly no art to be found.

In an effort to be liked, you are now liked by no one.

3/26/17

Hey Donald,

I've always despised welfare - for the rich.

It cost taxpayers over $3 million for each of the 5 times that you have gone to your resort in Florida since the election. On top of that, the local Palm Beach Sheriff's Department has had to shell out over a million dollars so far protecting you and your groupies.

The Secret Service needs an additional $60 million next year just to support your lifestyle. So an average family pays around $4,000 in taxes each year. That means 15,000 families are squandering their hard earned money to pay for your Florida trips and to cover your wife and kid at a separate location.

Then your boy Eric spends over $100,000 in taxpayer's money last month flying to Uruguay to promote your Trump brand. To add insult to injury, the Secret Service spent over $12,000 renting skis last week while your extended family was living it up in Aspen.

According to a report from International Business Times, at the rate you are going, you will spend more money on travel in your first year than Obama did in 8 years.

A few years ago you tweeted, "Obama's vacation is costing taxpayers millions of dollars---Unbelievable!"

3/27/17

Hey Donald,

It appears that you and your climate change deniers may be going to battle with California soon. You may be in for trouble.

The California Air Resources Board recently voted unanimously to confirm tighter emission standards for all vehicles in the state in an effort to reduce Co2, which in case you didn't know, contributes heavily to climate change. This is their right due to a waiver granted by the Clean Air Act, and since 12 other states follow California's rules, it affects a third of all cars on the road.

You vowed a couple of weeks ago while strutting around at an auto plant in Michigan, to loosen mileage and emission rules to help stimulate sales. Basically you want to throw a huge chunk of red meat to automakers at the expense of the environment.

Since the auto industry can't economically tailor their cars' emission rates to accommodate different states' requirements, and they are not about to give up a third of their sales, they want the rules changed so they can essentially make "one car fits all".

If you try to change CA's waiver, they will sue. And knowing Jerry Brown, the conflict will be epic. All major automakers supported tighter standards before you came along because Obama bailed out their industry. Now they smell blood.

3/28/17

Hey Donald,

Yesterday your diminutive Attorney General, Jeff Sessions, said this regarding Sanctuary Cities: "Unfortunately, some states and cities have adopted policies 'designed to frustrate' the enforcement of our immigration laws." Let that phrase sink in.

You want to withhold federal money to these cities that consciously make a decision within their limited budgets to not spend their taxpayers' dollars seeking out, apprehending, processing, and deporting undocumented immigrants. They would rather spend their money apprehending genuine thieves, rapists, and murderers, most of whom are not immigrants.

Tom Wong, a UC political scientist found that those cities that do not enforce ICE requests have lower crime rates than those who do. Look up the study and you will understand why.

Meanwhile regarding Obamacare, on your first night in office you directed the IRS to process returns without proof of health insurance as mandated by law. Then you yanked advertising that was already in place encouraging new enrollees to sign up. On top of that you said, "the best thing we can do politically speaking is let Obamacare explode."

So this sounds like you are taking actions "designed to frustrate" the success of the Affordable Care Act. Is that true?

3/29/17

Hey Donald,

The next chapter of Trumpgate seems to be unfolding. Devin Nunes, the Chairman of the Intelligence Committee, and a dairy farmer from CA (and your lap dog in the House), told you last week that Obama spied on you after all! You got all excited and tweeted out something like "I told you so!" Only it wasn't true.

Now I don't have anything against dairy farmers, but Nunes doesn't seem to know that he's entering treacherous legal waters. His counterpart, Adam Schiff, who has a Political Science degree from Stanford and a law degree from Harvard certainly does.

So after Schiff called Nunes out for his mad caper, Nunes had to crawl back and tell the committee he was sorry. Then we find out that he got his "news" from an operative inside the White House!!!

THEN, you and your people complained to Nunes about a hearing that was scheduled by his committee involving Sally Yates, the former Acting Attorney General, so he cancelled the hearing! She apparently had some answers to "what did you know and when did you know it?", regarding you and your associates' involvement in the Russian sabotage of our elections.

Sure looks like a cover-up to me.

3/30/17

Hey Donald,

Perhaps the most pernicious action you have taken so far in your corrupt presidency is your signing of an order on Tuesday that rolls back the Clean Power Plan, putting more carbon in the air.

There is almost complete consensus by climate scientists that human activity is raising the Earth's temperature. Half of the population believes in the science and the other half (including you) have been duped or bought off by the fossil fuel industry.

The Climate and Security Advisory Group, which is made up of 43 senior military and security experts, sent you a briefing book last fall. Here's what they wrote. "Stresses from climate change can increase the likelihood of international or civil conflict, state failure, mass migration and instability in strategically significant areas around the world."

Then there's this. According to Politico, a supervisor at the Energy Department's international climate office told staff this week not to use the phrases "climate change," "emissions reduction" or "Paris Agreement" in written memos, briefings or other written communication."

You've squandered the opportunity to lead the world on one of the most consequential challenges facing life here on Planet Earth.

3/31/17

Hey Donald,

Both the Senate and the House have now voted almost entirely along party lines to undo internet privacy rules adopted under the Obama administration. We know you don't use a computer, and consequently don't understand what's at stake here, but a lot of us get it. DO NOT SIGN THIS CHANGE INTO LAW.

The rules which were supposed to go into effect at the end of the year required that Internet providers get our permission before collecting and selling our "precise geo-location, financial information, health information, children's information, social security numbers, web browsing history, app usage history and the content of communications", according to the BBC.

Congress sold out to large Internet service providers like Verizon, Comcast, and AT&T, all of which have contributed hundreds of thousands of dollars to their campaigns. Even commentators on Bannon's Breitbart site have attacked this move.

A GoFundMe site has been set up to help buy and release the data of each politician who voted in favor of this measure. It's a long shot, but theoretically possible under the changes.

Imagine their surprise! This would be a classic case of "chickens coming room to roost".

4/1/17

Hey Donald,

It's April Fool's Day today - it seems that this holiday was made just for you! There are so many examples to choose from to support this notion, but here's one from yesterday. You tweeted:

"Mike Flynn should ask for immunity in that this is a witch hunt (excuse for big election loss), by media and Dems, of historic proportion!"

So how does the witch, Mike Flynn, asking for immunity have anything to do with the Democrats losing the election?

And do you really believe that the investigations by Congress and the FBI are punishment for you winning the election?

And do you really believe you won the election by historic proportions?

The truth is that your Electoral College victory ranked 46th out of 58 presidential elections.

And your popular vote deficit gave you the third worst vote margin among winning candidates in presidential elections since 1824.

You really are a fool, aren't you?

4/2/17

Hey Donald.

Climate change denier, and now your head of the EPA, Scott Pruitt, recently refused to ban a dangerous pesticide that risks human health. As you recall, he barely won Senate confirmation.

Chlorpyrifos, commonly known as Lorsban, has been used for years on strawberries, broccoli, citrus fruits, and many other foods. The EPA banned its indoor use more than 10 years ago.

Evidence suggests that fetuses that are exposed to this toxin risk brain and nervous system development. Scott Faber from the Environmental Working Group, said that, "the science is so strong, so overwhelming, that chlorpyrifos causes neurological problems." Obama proposed stopping the use of chlorpyrifos on food in response to a petition filed by the Natural Resources Defense Council and Pesticide Action Network North America.

A federal judge recently gave the EPA a deadline to decide whether to finalize its ban of the pesticide. Pruitt said no.

Dow Chemical, the maker of Lorsban, bought over a million dollar's worth of favor from politicians in 2016.

To put it simply, your EPA guy would rather stand by and allow corporations to profit at the expense of children's health.

4/3/17

Hey Donald,

Back in June, you fiercely went after Indiana born Judge Gonzalo Curiel, calling him out for his "Mexican heritage". It was a despicable and racist comment, made far worse by the fact that you are now the president and supposed to set an example for all of America, and indeed the world. You have failed miserably.

Last week Judge Curiel approved a $25 million settlement deal between you and the students you defrauded over your bogus Trump University scandal. Under the terms, you don't have to admit wrongdoing. Of course you were wrong! We all know it.

Back in 2016 you said this about the case, "I don't settle lawsuits. Probably should have settled it, but I just can't do that. Mentally I can't do it. I'd rather spend a lot more money and fight it."

According to USA Today, you have been involved in over 3,500 lawsuits in the last 30 years and you've been sued 60 times since you became president! People typically don't get sued if they don't do anything wrong. Just last week a judge allowed another suit to proceed, charging that you incited violence at one of your political rallies last year.

So I'm wondering how you will that feel when you sign that $25 million check. Will you have any remorse? I doubt it.

4/4/17

Hey Donald,

"Still nothing prepared us for the magnitude of this train wreck."

That line is from the second in a four part series about you that's running in the Los Angeles Times this week. There's more:

"It was no secret during the campaign that Donald Trump was a narcissist and a demagogue who used fear and dishonesty to appeal to the worst in American voters." And it goes on:

"What is most worrisome about Trump is Trump himself. He is a man so unpredictable, so reckless, so petulant, so full of blind self-regard, so untethered to reality that it is impossible to know where his presidency will lead or how much damage he will do to our nation. His obsession with his own fame, wealth and success, his determination to vanquish enemies real and imagined, his craving for adulation — these traits were, of course, at the very heart of his scorched-earth outsider campaign; indeed, some of them helped get him elected. But in a real presidency in which he wields unimaginable power, they are nothing short of disastrous."

And finally this: "Those who oppose the new president's reckless and heartless agenda must make their voices heard." We will, Mr. President. We will.

4/5/17

Hey Donald,

Your admiration for strongmen was on full display again Monday when you hosted a murderous dictator. You lavished him with praise, and never mentioned his abysmal human rights record.

Egypt's ruler Abdel Fattah el-Sisi has jailed over 60,000 people since his fraudulent election in 2014. His regime has built 16 new prisons to accommodate his political prisoners.

President Obama wouldn't let him near the White House, but you seem to be drawn to authoritarian figures and their tactics.

A year after the brutal crackdown of peaceful dissenters in Tiananmen Square in 1989, you told Playboy Magazine, "they put it down with strength. That shows you the power of strength." Last year you seemed amused by the way Saddam Hussein dealt with suspected terrorists saying, "A one day trial and shoot him...and the one day trial usually lasted five minutes, right?" Then in response to a question from Joe Scarborough about Putin last fall you said, "He's running his country, and at least he's a leader."

OK so eight prominent Russian dissidents have died mysteriously since November of last year, and 23 members of the media have been killed since 2000.

4/6/17

Hey Donald,

"You know, it doesn't really matter what [the media] write as long as you've got a young and beautiful piece of ass."

That's what you told Esquire magazine in 1991 in an interview.

There are dozens of other examples pertaining to your attitude toward women, with the most recent being on March 27th when you revoked Obama's 2014 "Fair Pay and Safe Workplaces" order. This rule ensured that companies with federal contracts complied with 14 labor and civil rights laws.

The Fair Pay order involved language regarding wage and salary transparency along with a ban on forced arbitration clauses for sexual assault, sexual harassment, or other discrimination claims.

In case you don't know, forced arbitration clauses (or cover-up clauses) are designed to sweep sexual harassment and other similar claims under the rug and keep them out of the courts. Obama's order brought these claims out into the open so everyone had a chance to see how employers treat their women employees.

Now corporations won't get busted for using their women employees for sex objects, while paying them less than men for doing the exact same job.

4/7/17

Hey Donald,

You bombed Syria after you saw the images on TV of dead and dying children poisoned with Sarin gas. Never mind that you warned Obama over a dozen times in 2013 not to do what you just did. You now have a war on your hands.

OK, so what about your own actions that will hasten the deaths of many of our children here in America and abroad?

Your EPA director plans to eliminate programs that limit children's exposure to lead based paint. Lead causes damage to young people's brains and nervous systems. Many will likely die early.

You are gutting the Clean Power Program that will dramatically affect children's health and their subsequent early demise.

You are allowing the continued use of chlorpyrifos, a pesticide which has been proven to cause brain damage in children.

You don't believe in man made climate change. Your inaction will hasten rising sea waters, resulting in the displacement of millions of people, famine, war, and civil strife - all of which will kill hundreds of thousands of kids along the way.

Are your policies your own version of Sarin gas?

4/8/17

Hey Donald,

History will judge whether or not you did the right thing in Syria. You reacted largely on emotion after seeing pictures on television, and emotion doesn't translate well into policy. You have none.

Meanwhile your legal fight continues to keep young Syrian children and their families who are exposed to similar atrocities out of this country.

According to UNICEF, the number of kids killed, injured, or recruited as child soldiers was "at its worst" in 2016. Over 650 children died in Syria last year because of the fighting and 850 more were forced to become executioners or suicide bombers - a 20% increase from the year before. 22 million Syrians have been displaced - that's half the country. Well over 200,000 Syrians have been killed and 2.3 million children are now refugees.

Last fall you said that banning Syrian refugees from our country was "a matter of quality of life".

By the way, according to your recent FEC disclosure, you owned or perhaps still own stock in Raytheon, the company that makes Tomahawk missiles that you launched on Syria.

The value of the company surged a billion dollars after the strike.

4/9/17

Hey Donald,

If your buddy, Senator Mitch McConnell, were my father, I would beg a stranger to adopt me, just so I could get away from this man. He's the most despicable politician since Joseph McCarthy.

McConnell said this shortly after the election of our first African American president, "The single most important thing we want to achieve is for President Obama to be a one-term president."

So then we lose Antonin Scalia. Almost before his body went cold, McConnell crowed that he would not even hold a hearing on Obama's nominee to fill the vacancy, arguing that it was too close to the election, even though there was precedent.

Here's what McConnell said in 2013 about Harry Reid after Republican's unprecedented obstruction of Obama's selections for Federal Court judgeships, "Breaking the rules to change the rules is un-American. I just hope the majority leader thinks about his legacy, the future of his party, and, most importantly, the future of our country before he acts."

So McConnell decides to becomes un-American too! It's one of the most audacious tits for tats in political history.

All I can say is that you owe McConnell a big hug and a kiss.

4/10/17

Hey Donald,

I am repeatedly disgusted by your behavior.

The latest example is your audible defense of your friend and mentor Bill O'Reilly, who was recently accused of sexual harassment by five women. Fox has already paid out $13 million in hush money to them, and advertisers are fleeing his show like pigeons at a shooting range. He is now under investigation.

You called O'Reilly "a good person" and went so far as to say, "I don't think Bill did anything wrong." Of course - in your mind, sexual harassment is perfectly OK. After all, you are our Predator in Chief. As a reminder, replay the infamous Billy Bush tape.

You just declared that this is 'sexual assault awareness month', and that we need to "protect vulnerable groups." Empty words….

Then there's Roger Ailes who cost Fox News $20 million to settle just one claim! He allegedly harassed multiple women but you felt "very badly" for Ailes and said that "some of the women that are complaining, I know how much he's helped them."

So if a man helps further a women's career, he then has the right to sexually assault her?

You are today's modern day version of Caligula.

4/11/17

Hey Donald,

Everyone knows you have absolutely no idea what you are doing with Syria, but at least you should get your stories straight.

This past Sunday, former Exxon boss and Putin admirer turned Secretary of State, said that your strike on Syria, "was related solely to the most recent horrific use of chemical weapons….other than that, there is no change to our military posture."

But then Nikki Haley, former Governor turned UN Ambassador, said, "there's not any sort of option where a political solution is going to happen with Assad at the head of the regime. Regime change is something that we think is going to happen…."

But last month she said, your priority in Syria, "is no longer to sit there and focus on getting Assad out." She said the conflict would be resolved by the Syrian people. John McCain thinks that Assad gassed his own people again because of statements like this.

After Assad first used chemical weapons in 2013, you urged Obama not to retaliate, saying it would "bring nothing but trouble."

Well there's trouble now. You guys are in such disarray that you aren't even talking to each other, let alone know what the next steps are. Good luck with that.

4/12/17

Hey Donald,

I am really glad that you don't drink. If you went on regular benders, the nightmares many of us are now experiencing, would be like counting sheep in comparison.

Henry Kissinger recounted that your idol Richard Nixon would get s**t faced and then threaten military action against his enemies late at night. According to historians, when the North Koreans downed one of our spy planes in 1969, Nixon ordered a nuclear strike in retaliation. Kissinger knew he was soused, so he told the top brass to hang loose until Nixon slept it off. Obviously Nixon reconsidered over coffee the next morning.

Then there was the happy drunk, Boris Yeltsin, the former president of Russia. In 1995 he got totally wasted at the White house and was found outside late at night in his underwear trying to hail a cab. He said he was in the mood for pizza. The next night he overindulged again and the Secret Service almost took him down thinking he was an intruder trying to get inside the guest house where he was staying. Another time when he was three sheets to the wind at a banquet, Yeltsin used the bald head of the president of Kyrgyzstan as a drum, with spoons as drumsticks.

Something tells me though that if you drank, you would be more like Nixon than Yeltsin. With that, thank you for being a teetotaler.

4/13/17

Hey Donald,

What do you think these countries have in common:
Mali, Yemen, Sudan, Niger, Chad, Eritrea, Djibouti,
Nigeria, Ethiopia, South Sudan, Somalia, Central
African Republic, and Cameroon?

I can tell you. More than 20 million of their citizens
are starving - and angry. And when people are mad
and hungry, they do desperate things like join
revolutions, which often results in terrorism. No one
likes to watch their child starve to death.

You watched little children dying from Sarin gas on TV
and became all emotional. That's fine - we all did.
But why don't you have the same reaction to little
children who are dying by the thousands each day
because they have nothing to eat? Their suffering
lasts for years in comparison until their little bodies
give up. Is it because they're not on FOX TV, which is
apparently where most of your information comes
from? Try PBS sometime.

In 1961, President Kennedy said, "Food is strength,
and food is peace, and food is freedom, and food is a
helping to people around the world whose good will
and friendship we want."

Your proposed budget will strip funding for
International Food Aid Programs. Meanwhile, 1.25
million children will starve to death this year, and
terrorism will flourish. It makes no sense at all.

4/14/17

Hey Donald,

Betsy DeVos, your multibillionaire Education Secretary, recently ripped up a couple of memorandums from the Obama administration that were designed to help students manage or help figure out ways to discharge their debt through various means. She caved to lobbyists of the loan servicing industry.

The government subs out management of its loans to private contractors. Before Obama came to office, these contracts were awarded to those firms that were good at collecting money, no matter how vicious they were in the process. Obama changed the rules which resulted in more contracts going to companies that were sensitive to borrowers needs.

Navient Corp. is among the finalists for a contract in 2019 after the current ones expire. They are being sued by 2 states for abusing borrowers in order to increase profits. Shares of the company skyrocketed after the news of the police change.

According to the Center for American Progress, DeVos's action "will certainly increase the likelihood of default."

Currently students owe over a trillion dollars to the government in loans. It's a huge economic bubble about to burst, and DeVos just sped up the process by favoring corporations over students.

4/15/17

Hey Donald,

You wouldn't release your tax returns so we could see how much you gamed the system, or how closely tied you are to the Russian Mafia. Now you won't let us see who you are letting into the White House. Just a few years ago you tweeted, "Why is Barack Obama spending millions to try and hide his records? He is the least transparent President--ever--and he ran on transparency."

You said you were going to "drain the swamp", but instead you are hiding visits by lobbyists, political donors, corporate executives, and everyone else trying to get your ear. How many Russian Oligarchs have you invited in? How about Dmitry Rybolovlev, who's been following you around, and who bought that moldy mansion from you in 2008 for double its value?

So you're being sued for those records, which I support. We have a right to know what our president is up to.

You also decided to trash open.whitehouse.gov, which not only would reveal the ne'er-do-wells that you host, but also how much we are paying your "yes" people. They called the site a waste of taxpayer money and that ending it would save $70,000 by 2020. Meanwhile you've spent $80 million of our money traveling to your Florida getaway - that's $1 million a day since the inauguration.

3/16/17

Hey Donald,

It's Easter Sunday, which reminds me again of the wide support you continue to receive from "so called" Christians. It illustrates the appalling hypocrisy that exists within the 81% of the Christian community who voted for you. I believe they have squandered their values.

Real Christians have always celebrated morality and truth - they are two of the most fundamental tenants of Christianity and supported by multiple Biblical passages.

Take Revelation 21:8, for example:.... the sexually immoral....the idolaters and all liars—they will be consigned to the fiery lake of burning sulfur." If there's a hell, Donald, you're in serious trouble.

We all know that you're morally challenged and lying is an integral part of who you are. Why would bonafide Christians sacrifice their own truth and morality by supporting a person like you? Using you solely for the Supreme Court is a pathetic sellout. This country needs a serious leader and a serious thinker, and you are neither.

North Carolina Pastor John Pavlovitz writes that your lifestyle is "exactly the kind of greedy, bloated, bitter, violent, self-centered, myopic existence that Jesus spent his life calling us to reject."

4/17/17

Hey Donald,

Your policies are prioritizing profits over lives. In other words, you are killing American workers.

Crystalline silica is a carcinogenic dust that's given off when sand and granite are processed in the construction industry, or the sand itself is used for blasting. The dangers of this dust have been known since the Roosevelt Administration, and just last year, Obama was finally able to tighten the rules pertaining to the use of silica. The effort to get that far took 45 years, and experts in the field regarded the changes as lifesaving.

Just recently your people said that they were going to delay the implementation of these new regulations for at least 3 months and potentially a lot longer. I strongly urge you to reconsider.

Building trades groups have sued the government to stop the new rules from going into effect, and you are are once again kowtowing to greedy corporations instead of real people. Companies that would be affected by the changes are whining about the costs. How much is a life worth to you anyway?

The Occupational Safety and Health Administration said that the new rules would reduce silica exposure for over 2 million people, preventing around 600 deaths per year.

4/18/17

Hey Donald,

Washington Post reporter David Fahrenthold was awarded a Pulitzer Prize recently for uncovering your "locker-room banter" - or in other words, your bragging about being a sex offender.

He also discovered that you didn't donate the money you promised to veterans groups after a fundraiser in Iowa until you got called out. You were going to quietly hang on to it.

Fahrenthold found out too that you hadn't contributed to your Donald J. Trump foundation since 2008, but instead asked others to cough up - and you bought things for yourself with the money - like Tim Tebow's helmet for $12,000 and 2 giant paintings of yourself for $30,000. AND that you used $258,000 of foundation money to settle lawsuits involving some of your for-profit companies.

He also let us know about your $25,000 bribe to Florida Attorney General Pam Bondi, which resulted in her not joining a fraud investigation into your bogus Trump University.

So what kind of a person takes money from people who think that it's going to a good cause and then spends if for themselves?

David Fahrenthold proved to us that you have no conscience.

4/19/17

Hey Donald,

Your daughter, Ivanka is using your office to get rich - or rather, richer. In fact, you and your entire family have turned The White House into a for-profit cesspool.

You were all over China from the beginning - branding them as currency manipulators, challenging the "One China" policy, taking an unprecedented call from Taiwan etc. Essentially you poked them in the eye repeatedly.

So a couple of weeks ago you and Ivanka, along with her husband Jared, had dinner with the president of China at your resort in Florida. Not so coincidentally on the same day, China approved several of Ivanka's trademarks, which gave her company a monopoly over there with these items. 23 more trademarks are pending such as handbags, clothing lines, software, skin care lotions, and other products.

Her two companies - The Ivanka Trump Collection and IvankaTrump.com are worth around $50 million and growing.

Meanwhile you're attitude toward China has shifted dramatically now that there's money to be made.

4/20/17

Hey Donald,

In January you promised to address cybersecurity saying, "I will appoint a team to give me a plan within 90 days of taking office." Today is your 90th day in office and there is no team and no plan. You've been too busy blaming others for your failures.

A major cyberattack on our country is one of the largest threats we face and experts in this field believe that it's imminent. Drones can be hijacked and used against our military, hospitals could go dark and life saving machines rendered useless, the power grid can be taken out causing air traffic to come to a standstill, financial markets can collapse, and personal information would be stolen on a scale bigger than ever before.

To be fair, you did hastily prepare an executive order dealing with this issue toward the end of January with an announcement saying, "We must protect federal networks and data. We operate these networks on behalf of the American people and they are very important." Then you pulled the order and signed nothing. You must have abruptly realized - again - that things like this are complicated. You were obviously clueless.

The election last fall was sabotaged because of a breach in cybersecurity and you came out on top thanks to the Russians. Next time they might pick a more favorable candidate.

4/21/17

Hey Donald,

You're doing some really important things these days!
I noticed that Kid Rock, Sarah Palin, and Ted Nugent
dropped by for a visit yesterday! These dignitaries are
all well known for their wholesome lifestyles and their
excellent advice, so they are certainly in keeping with
the respectful nature of the Oval Office.

Did Sarah reminisce about the night she and her
family were involved in a drunken brawl a few years
ago? According to the Anchorage Police Dept., the
cops were called to a "verbal and physical altercation"
at a house where "some of the Palin family members
were in attendance at the party." Apparently Sarah's
daughter Bristol and her son Track know how to fight!
Even husband Todd supposedly ended up with a
bloody nose! Quite the story! I hope she shared it
with you.

Say did Kid Rock bring you one of his vulgar tee
shirts? He's been promoting them online. If he
forgot, you can order one here:
http://kidrock.warnerbrosrecords.com/apparel.html

Oh and did Ted Nugent tell you about the time he was
visited by the Secret Service? During one of his
concerts a few years ago, he waved an assault rifle
and said this about Hillary Clinton: she should "ride
one of these into the sunset, you worthless bitch". He
also said Obama should "suck on my machine gun."

4/22/17

Hey Donald,

Thousands of scientists and their supporters around the world will be marching today to highlight the the growing disregard for evidence based research. Each walker will be thinking of you, and I'm afraid they won't necessarily be good thoughts.

Did you ask the President of China when you met with him recently about the "Climate Change Hoax" that they invented? Did you brag to him that you had any reference to climate change removed from The White House website?

You also told the EPA that you were going to halt their grants and contracts to study environmental issues. You've also muzzled the Interior Department and the Dept. of Agriculture, telling them to keep their mouths shut when it comes to science.

Oh, just for good measure, your Attorney General Jeff Sessions recently said that he would abandon the National Commission on Forensic Science. This means that more innocent people will likely be executed for crimes they did not commit.

On another note, I've often wondered if you had your kids vaccinated when they were little. I'm guessing you did.

Do any of them have autism?

4/23/17

Hey Donald,

During your campaign, you called the Iran Nuclear Agreement, "the dumbest deal perhaps I've ever seen in the history of deal-making. My number-one priority is to dismantle the disastrous deal with Iran." Like most issues, you had no idea what was in it. It was simply another example of Obama bashing that you used to divide our country, and scare people into voting for you.

Back in March of 2016 while speaking to AIPAC, you said, "I've studied this issue in great detail — I would say actually greater by far than anybody else." The entire audience laughed at you, knowing full well that you don't read.

Now you are grudgingly accepting the fact that the deal is working and that you cannot make a better one. Like this and many other issues, smarter people than you have had to set you straight.

This agreement among several of our allies took years, and involved some of the sharpest diplomats, engineers, and technicians in the world. Obama even insisted that Energy Secretary Ernest Moniz be part of the team because of his extensive background as a renowned nuclear physicist.

Donald, you're idea of a good deal is to not pay people for goods and services they provided to your businesses over the years.

4/24/17

Hey Donald,

North Korea has the world's fourth largest army, 21,000 artillery guns - many aimed at South Korea and American soldiers stationed there - and they have thousands of tons of chemical weapons. General Gary Luk who used to command our forces in South Korea says that a war there would cost $1 trillion and could kill a million people or more.

Right now, the USS Carl Vinson is headed toward the Korean Peninsula with Japan conducting joint exercises with the United States. North Korea said today that this was "an extremely dangerous act by those who plan a nuclear war to invade".

We all know there aren't too many options, so it's going to take some really smart people to deal with this looming threat. I really hope you listen to them. Jieun Baek recently published a book called, "North Korea's Hidden Revolution", in which she talks about undermining their regime by smuggling in more information about their leaders and about the outside world - in other words the idea of sowing discontent from within. Think outside the box.

You spoke with both the Chinese President and Japan's Prime Minister this morning and they are telling you to be careful. This is not the time to show off. One careless move on your part and the course of human history on Planet Earth will be changed forever.

3/25/17

Hey Donald,

Sonny Perdue's nomination for Agricultural Secretary was confirmed on Monday, even though he was accused of 13 ethics violations while serving as the governor of Georgia.

In 2002, he violated Georgia law when he funneled large amounts of money from his business into his campaign, and in 2005 he was fined for failing to report donations. He also gave cushy government jobs to business associates and campaign donors. In 2004, his lawyer intervened in legislation that gave Perdue a tax break of $100,000 on Florida land that he owned.

You have proposed a 20% reduction in spending for the USDA, including deep cuts to Nutritional Assistance to Women and Children. Have you talked to Perdue about cuts to welfare for large scale farming operations too?

Take a look at: https://farm.ewg.org/index.php. This data base will show you how much each farmer in the US receives in taxpayer dollars each year in the form of "assistance", or rather....welfare. Members of Congress hauled in at least $9.5 million in farm subsidies between 1995 and 2014.

In 2006 Perdue said, "we trust in the Lord for rain and many other things." Presumably this means free taxpayer money as well.

4/26/17

Hey Donald,

These cringeworthy quotes are from your recent interview:

"Well, the one thing I would say–and I say this to people–I never realized how big it was. Everything's so like, you know, the orders are so massive. I was talking to–Number one, there's great responsibility. The financial cost of everything is so massive, every agency. This is thousands of times bigger, the United States, than the biggest company in the world. ... It's massive! And every agency is, like, bigger than any company. So, you know, I really just see the bigness of it all."

"I don't watch CNN anymore. ... They treat me so badly. No, I just said that. No, I–What'd I say?–I stopped watching them!"

"People want the border wall. My base definitely wants the border wall. My base really wants it....OK, the thing they want more than anything is the wall. My base, which is a big base. I think my base is 45 percent. You know? It's funny."

"I have, it's interesting, I have, seem to get very high ratings. I definitely. You know....I have all the ratings for all those morning shows. When I go, they go double, triple....". Donald, do you know why? People are in awe of catastrophe....

4/27/17

Hey Donald,

By the end of this week, you will have signed 32 executive orders, which is the most of any president in their first 100 days since World War II. At a town hall last year you said this: "The country wasn't based on executive orders....Obama goes around signing executive orders...it's a basic disaster. You can't do it."

One of the most recent is your order to force the Interior Dept. to review national monument designations. You said, "The Antiquities Act does not give the federal government unlimited power to lock up millions of acres of land and water, and it's time we ended this abusive practice...now we're going to free it up."

Abusive practice? Monument designations take many years to develop and involve thousands of people. Most of these lands are already controlled by the public - monument designation merely ensures that the land is not exploited by the fossil fuel industry.

You said, "Tremendously positive things are going to happen on that incredible land, the likes of which there is nothing more beautiful anywhere in the world, but now tremendously positive things will happen."

Yes Donald, in your mind, "tremendously positive things" mean oil derricks, open pit coal mines, fracking operations, and fat wallets.

4/28/17

Hey Donald,

Your Attorney General, Jeff Sessions thinks marijuana is as dangerous as heroin and wants it eradicated. If he chooses to take on the industry, his efforts will likely lead to full legalization.

Get this: 61% of Americans want pot to be fully legal, 94% say doctors should be able to prescribe it, 73% think the states where pot is legal should be left alone, recreational marijuana is legal in 8 states, medical marijuana is legal in 22 states where together 200 million people live, as much as $20 billion is spent each year on prohibition, and finally, 40 million people are regular users.

If Sessions decides to launch a War on Weed, he will lose. Imagine the videos of armed federal officers smashing down state sanctioned operations and hauling their owners and employees off to jail. If they want to keep their jobs, Republican and Democratic legislators will have no choice but to take up the matter once and for all and make pot legal across the board. Reefer madness will be over. Maybe this is just what we need.

Sessions said the Ku Klux Klan "was OK until I found out they smoked pot" and that "good people don't smoke marijuana."

If this is true, there are really a lot of bad people in this country.

4/29/17

Hey Donald,

This is my 100th letter to you since your Inauguration 100 days ago. I have yet to get a response from The White House.

Each letter has been about an issue I feel strongly about, whether it was your unfitness for the highest office in the land, your lack of understanding of how government works, your inability to tell fact from fiction, or your lack of deep convictions. It's all about you.

Barack Obama's tenure as President exposed the underbelly of racism in this country, and you exploited that condition by bringing hatred out into the open, making our country more divided than ever. Your campaign rallies were filled with vile, and you catered to the worst instincts in people. Yet our system elected you.

As president, you sold out immediately to the "establishment" and corporate elitists, and you have already forgotten the very people who voted for you, and who trusted that you would somehow make their lives better. You are completely self centered and your style of governing is based on fear. America was a great country already, but you are making it worse.

I feel sorry for our nation and in a sense, for you. I believe that deep inside you are a pathetic, small, insecure boy, wanting to be liked.